THE PENGUIN PRINCIPLE

[A Little Story About
True Teamwork]

Antarctic Mike

INDIE BOOKS
INTERNATIONAL

ISBN: 1-941870-34-1
ISBN 13: 978-1-941870-34-1
Library of Congress Control Number: 2015941569

Designed by Joni McPherson, mcphersongraphics.com

INDIE BOOKS INTERNATIONAL, LLC
2424 VISTA WAY, SUITE 316
OCEANSIDE, CA 92054

www.indiebooksintl.com

CONTENTS

A NOTE FROM THE AUTHOR

> ## The Penguin Principle:
> True teamwork
> is putting the needs of others
> before your own.

When you think of true teamwork, what comes to your mind? For me, I'll never forget the day the underdog 1980 United States Olympic ice hockey team won the gold medal.

This was not only one of the greatest sports moments ever, but it was one of the best examples of true teamwork functioning at the highest level we'll ever see. "On paper" they were not the most talented. They were not the fastest, strongest or even a close favorite to medal, yet alone win the gold. Against all odds, these underdogs accomplished what many teams dream of and few achieve.

In the 2004 film *Miracle*, Kurt Russell stars as coach Herb Brooks in the true story of that 1980 USA Olympic ice hockey team winning the gold medal by defeating the powerful Soviet Union and Finland teams at Lake Placid, New York. Brooks had a dream of coaching the USA Olympic team ever since he was cut as a player from the 1960 USA Olympic team.

Brooks's dream comes true, and he gets the coaching gig in 1979. He puts together a team of college kids and begins to get them into shape. Since the Soviet Union is the greatest hockey team in the world, Brooks begins to retrain his team in the European style of playing the game. These USA college kids were true underdogs, because the "top dog" Soviet Union team had won four consecutive gold medals and had recently defeated a team of National Hockey League all-stars.

Brooks said that the problem with the NHL all-stars was that they were individual players and not a true team. With all his hard training, he finally turns the Americans into a team and a family. In a Cinderella story, the USA team defeats the Soviet Union in the semifinal round by not allowing

A NOTE FROM THE AUTHOR

them a single goal for the last ten minutes of the game, and then finished off powerful Finland in the final.

With the world watching the game on TV, sportscaster Al Michaels asks his famous question at the end of the game, "Do you believe in miracles? Yes!"

There were many keys to that miracle on ice, but in the end it came down to one thing. Each of the individuals cared more about their teammates than they did about themselves. They played their hearts out for the team, for the other players, for their coaches, and for their fans, but not for themselves. A team that plays at that level so selflessly is easy to admire, yet difficult to imitate in the world of business.

However, there is a greater underdog team that takes to the ice and executes at high levels. Unlike the 1980 hockey Olympians, this is one team you probably would not picture if you were asked to think of a great team.

This team is not a sports team, a business team or a professional association. This team is not made up of people and very few of us have ever witnessed them in action. Yet they have as much to teach us about being a great team as any group that exists in the world.

In fact, to see this team in action, you have to travel very far. They are the Emperor penguins who live in Antarctica, the true miracle on ice.

Perhaps you witnessed these magnificent creatures in the 2005 Academy Award-winning movie, *March of the Penguins*. With narration by Morgan Freeman, the film is a look at the annual journey of emperor penguins as they march—single file— to their traditional breeding ground. In my trips to Antarctica I have had the privilege to observe these amazing birds that I call the world's best performing team in the worst conditions on earth.

The struggle to survive gave the penguins the ten gifts of true teamwork. But how did it all begin? This is a little fable with an important message for every organization in the world. May the ten gifts of *The Penguin Principle* bring you the benefits of true teamwork.

Antarctic Mike
June, 2015

PROLOGUE: ALL THIS IS TRUE

"Antarctica used to be a tropical place densely forested and teeming with life. But then the continent started to drift south. And by the time it was done drifting, the dense forests had all been replaced with a new ground cover — ice. As for the former inhabitants, they had all died or moved on long ago. Well, almost all of them. Legend has it that one tribe stayed behind. Perhaps they thought the change in weather was only temporary. Or maybe they were just stubborn. But whatever their reasons, these stalwart souls refused to leave. For millions of years they have made their home on the darkest, driest, windiest and coldest continent on Earth. And they've done so pretty much alone. So in some ways this is a story of survival. A tale of life over death. But it's more than that, really. This is a story about love."

From the 2005 Academy Award-winning film,
March of the Penguins

Around sixty million years ago, back around the time of the dinosaurs, penguins were the size of people. And they could fly.

In those days, Antarctica was still comparatively warm.

As a result, the land held a great many creatures in addition to themselves, all of whom were hungry. And penguin chicks were very easy to catch and eat.

The original people of Australia, the Aborigines, have tales about how the animals and the world came to be. They call these legends of the "dream time." In these tales, all things—animals, people, even trees and the sun and the moon—can speak and act.

Animals, too, have their own versions of tales of the dream time.

THE MANTRA OF THE PENGUINS

What is The Penguin Principle?

We give all we have.

To whom do we give it?

Each other, even before ourselves.

Why?

So there may always be penguins,

every season, one after the other,

for all the seasons of all time.

STORY TIME IN MODERN DAY IN ANTARCTICA

> In which a modern mother begins to tell
> youngsters an ancient tale of the last penguins
> on Earth, and in so doing, starts to relay The
> Penguin Principle.

The light of the sun sliced through the Antarctic autumn day, reflecting off the ice in near-blinding blades that shimmered with a kind of warmth, if you could call it that when you were standing on a glacier.

A group of penguin chicks, nearly grown, were in the middle of shedding their soft baby down feathers and could feel the sun's warmth especially intensely in the spots where their shiny new black feathers had come in.

Near the place where the ice met the sea, a rowdy group of youngsters was showing off their new grown-up look—and tottering perilously close to the edge.

"Get back over here this *instant!*" rang a stern maternal voice across the glacier. "If you think your father and I nearly *starved* for *months* and almost *froze* to *death* in *blizzards* and came *thiiiiiis* close to exhaustion trudging *back* and *forth* and finally *hatched* you and *raised* you and kept you *safe* all *summer* long only to see you *fall* into the *sea* before you can *swim* and *drown* or get *eaten* by a *seal* or an *orca*, young man..."

The youngsters, led by an especially sheepish young fledgling, waddled over to the mother.

"I'm sorry, Mama," muttered the youngling. "It's only that these feathers are so different, and we were enjoying how they feel. They're so smooth and thick and long and warm in the sun, and now our faces are starting to look like yours and Papa's with yellow and orange!"

"Do you know how we penguins got these feathers in the first place? Do you know how we came to look like this? Hmmm? Do you know what it *took*? Do you know what *sacrifices* it required for you to be standing there at the edge of the ice, about to fall into water, after everything every penguin in this colony has given to make sure you're standing there enjoying your new multicolored faces?" asked the mother.

All the young penguins' heads hung bowed, just a little.

"No, Mother."

"Would you like to know?"

Tiny little penguin toes drew tiny little invisible circles on the ice.

"Yes, Mother."

The mother, raising herself up to her full height, nearly three-and-a-half feet tall, looked them over. Her gaze softened. She sighed.

"Soon you will all be ready to go to the sea yourselves. When you do, you will take with you this story. Every penguin does. Every penguin always has, since the beginning. Since the first year. One day you will tell it to the chicks of your colony, after your First Egg Time—but only when they are ready."

"It is the story of The Penguin Principle."

"What's The Penguin Principle?" a youngster asked.

"Of all the lessons you will ever learn, The Penguin Principle is the most important. It's the key to how we Emperor Penguins live our lives, work as a true team at the highest and survive here in the most challenging conditions in the world, where almost no other creature can."

And she raised her head and began to sing.

Long ago before we came together

Our ancient ancestors faced the Egging Time alone

The predators made meals of chicks and mothers

The fathers did not see, for they had gone

Until one day not many penguins lingered

Our numbers down to just a starving few

They gathered near the sea and pulled together

And off to Center Island Arthur flew—

"Wait, what!?" a young fledgling interrupted, with wide eyes. "What do you mean he flew? We do not fly."

"Hush and listen, young one. Patience is a gift."

She chuckled. That was the part of the song where every mother-singer always found herself interrupted, and a good thing too, because that was all there was to that particular penguin song. The mother settled in to tell the rest of the tale.

THE TALE OF ARTHUR THE PENGUIN AND THE MOON

That year so very long ago, none of the chicks who hatched survived long enough for their grown-up feathers to come in. This happened because of the Old Ways.

Back then, when penguins came out of the sea at Egging Time, every male and every female sought out a mate right then and there, the very hour they emerged, practically at the edge of the water. And there was no singing, no celebration. When they had chosen, they flew away, to find a secret spot, to build nests, far away from all the other penguins. They thought being alone would help them hide and be safe.

The chicks looked at each other, horrified. "Alone? All alone?"

"All alone," said the mother, nodding sadly. "Now you see how it came to be that we almost came to our end. Penguins can do nothing alone.

Instead of keeping us safe, splitting up into pairs and nesting alone was making us weaker. Every year, from every direction, the predators came. Like today, from the water came seals. From the air came skuas. But in those days, there were also very large predators we no longer see—giant things with scales and legs, and snakes and other creatures as well. Oh, yes, there were terrible creatures of all kinds here in ancient times.

"Why?" asked a young penguin.

Because of an ancient fight between the Sun and the Moon. You see, the Sun and the Moon are sisters, and they have a terrible rivalry. They cannot cooperate. They argue constantly over who will control the land and they will not share. Neither will give an inch.

Back then it was even worse, if you can believe that, because one day long before anybody was alive, the Sun crept up and caught the Moon sleeping. So she used a strong net and ropes to tie her sister up and drag her away. She tied her down to a large rock, deep in a cave, right here in the middle of this land. And then she rolled another large rock in front of the entrance to the cave, to make certain the Moon could not get out.

That was the beginning of a very long warm time in the world. The whole land came into bloom with life for many, many years. All the plants and the animals of Earth came into being during the Long Summer when the Moon was imprisoned.

All the animals the whole world over know this story.

They also know the story of how the Moon escaped, and at what price.

Anyway, back to that horrible year.

With just a handful of penguins left alive in the whole world, and predators coming to take our chicks from every side, only a few chicks had made it through Egging Time. Of those who were not taken and eaten during the Laying and the Hatching, some of the last survivors fell into the water before they could swim.

The modern mother looked pointedly at her own chick, who squirmed.

Now it was nearly Egging Time again, and still the Long Summer reigned, and all the predators smiled.

The remaining penguins—just a small number—gathered. They talked and debated for a long time. Then they agreed. Arthur, the wisest and most level-headed penguin of all, would go to the center of this land, to its very heart, and try to find the Moon.

Arthur would see if the Moon could help us.

So Arthur spread his great, bulky wings and began to fly.

It was a long, hard journey. Arthur flew for many days, crisscrossing the land, looking for the secret hiding place. He grew tired many times and had to return to the sea to eat. One day his search had been so exhausting and the flight back so long, he was so hungry, he was about to dive straight from the air into the water just as he arrived.

But a seagull nearby called "Stop! Stop! I saw a seal slip into the water just seconds ago!" So Arthur was spared.

"Thank you, Seagull," Arthur said. "I will remember this kindness all my days."

"You'd better, Lucky Penguin," said the seagull. "Might be that we meet again someday."

Finally, one day Arthur found himself flying over the center of the continent, where he entered the terrifying heart of the deepest forest, and there he found the mouth of a very cold cave. He found a small crack between the boulder blocking the cave opening and the wall of the mountain, and he wiggled through.

Inside it was very dark, but he knew he was in the right place, because he could see faint light in the distance, and he could also see his breath in the light. It was colder in the cave than anything he had ever felt in his life.

He called out.

"Hello? Is there anybody here?"

Nobody knows what the Moon's voice sounds like, but she answered him. And he followed her voice deep into the cave.

When he found her, chained and bound, Arthur asked the Moon, "If I release you, will you help us? We are dying. No matter where we go, no matter how hard we try to hide, our chicks are found and killed and eaten. We need to be alone."

"I can help you, but are you sure?" asked the Moon. "Alone? You wish to be left alone on this land?"

"Yes! If there are no predators on this land, we will be able to raise our chicks!"

"I can do this for you," said the Moon. "But it will come at a very high price. My sister the Sun will be very angry at you and your people. I will be able to help you when I am back in my rightful place, during the dark season, when the nights are longer than the days. But I cannot protect you during the season when she rules. During that time you will have to stay out of her sight. And you will never again be safe from her wrath in the sky."

Arthur removed the chains and bindings from the Moon. Then the Moon and Arthur spent three days talking in the cave about how he could remove the stone that was blocking the entrance to the cave, and what would happen next.

The Moon told Arthur that, after she fought her sister for her rightful place in the sky, she would break off the land from where it sat now and send it far to the south. That would bring dark and cold many months of the year. During her season, the waters would freeze and turn to enormous sheets of ice. Almost all the predators would flee the land or die.

"But there are still orcas and sea lions and skua," said one of the young penguins who was hanging on every word. "My Mama warned me about all of them."

No place is perfect.

At any rate, Arthur knew he could not free the Moon by himself. So after he made the deal with the Moon, he went to look for help. Arthur left the cave through the tiny opening he'd come through in the first place and started to circle in the sky. After a while, he saw a great giant creature that used to live in this land—a huge beast, as large as a whale, that stood tall on its legs. It was eating a kind of land-algae that used to cover the ground here, when it was still very warm.

Arthur tricked the land beast. He told it there were many, many more land-algae plants inside the cave.

He might have even told the land beast they were magical. Nobody is quite sure what Arthur said to the land beast. Only that what he said made the giant land beast very eager to move the huge rock away from the mouth of the cave, and so it used its mighty strength to do so.

Arthur cried into the cave, "Now, Moon, you are free!" and whoosh, the Moon came flying out and soared high into the sky!

The land beast, of course, did not find any more land algae in the cave and would have probably stomped on Arthur in anger if Arthur hadn't already flown away.

And that is when the Sky Sisters started to fight, and all the animals that used to live in this land started to run away.

The young penguins settled in for the rest of the story.

CHAPTER 1

THE ICE: THE GIFT OF MEANINGFUL PURPOSE

In which the last penguins on Earth receive The Gift of Meaningful Purpose from an unexpected benefactor...in an unexpected place...with the help of unexpected allies.

The day Arthur returned to the place where he had left the rest of the last penguins on Earth, the Moon returned to the sky.

And she was understandably very angry with her sister the Sun. The two began to fight while all the animals below stood and stared upward.

Well, almost all the animals. All the animals except the penguins.

Arthur landed at the edge of the sea just as the Great War between the Sun and the Moon was beginning. The land shook and rocked. The penguins were afraid, but he raised his beak and sang to call the penguins to him.

"Father, what happened? I can tell you must have found the Moon, but how can this help us?" asked Arthur's son Percy.

"Yes, what have you done!?" cried Roddy, a pessimistic penguin who could always be counted on to look under every chunk of ice and find droppings, and then drape them in black for extra measure. "Surely the end of the world is at hand!"

Arthur lowered his head and his voice and shushed the band of penguins. All around them were the murmurs and cries of all the other animals who were caught up in confusion as the two heavenly sisters fought for control of the sky once more.

"I found the Moon in her prison," he told the penguins. "And I asked her to help us, as we all agreed."

"I don't see a lot of help happening up there right now," interrupted Edmund, who was a bold, brash penguin who always lept before he looked and could be counted on never to lift a wing without first asking, "What's in it for me?" "We're just a few birds, and she's the Moon! You probably just made her and the Sun angry enough to kill every living thing! I knew this was a stupid plan! I wouldn't have gone along with it if you'd told us all exactly what you were planning to do in the first place!"

Other penguins began to nod and whisper in agreement with Edmund as the warring sisters continued their chaotic melee in the sky. It seemed, in fact, that Edmund could always be found at the center of any brewing discontent.

Arthur stood patiently while the penguins argued and harrumphed among themselves for a moment or two.

When there was a particularly loud crash from above and lurch from below, which knocked the penguins off balance and startled them into stunned silence, Arthur asked, "Shall I go on?"

They finally settled down. Arthur related the whole tale of what had happened in the cave when he and Seagull had met the Moon.

"We will give all we have to give. That is the promise I made," Arthur concluded.

"What do we have to give?" asked Roddy, suspicious and still unconvinced, as the thunder above and the lurching below continued. A couple of the penguins had lost their footing and fallen over once or twice already. Some of the other animals were fleeing deeper toward land, while others had already dived into the sea to get away from the warring sky sisters.

Arthur continued, "Today is the last day we will ever fly. We will trade the air for the sea. I offered the Moon this: Take our wings and make us the best swimmers in this sea. We will spend the Sun's season in the water, where she cannot see or reach us, and she cannot take her revenge. We will come ashore to make our eggs and raise our chicks during the Moon's season, when no other animal will dare to come and take them from us. She will protect us."

The uproar that erupted among the penguins at that point nearly matched the uproar going on in the sky. It took hours to die down. There was shouting, crying, keening and weeping, and why not?

The penguins' ways were ancient. For generations they had been birds of the air and the water. This agreement would change everything they had ever known or done.

Off a little way from the rest of the penguins, Arthur spoke with Ada, who was a penguin as level-headed, calm and clear-eyed as he was wise. They had had a chick together years before—Percy.

"They are upset, Arthur, but this is why we all agreed to send you in the first place," she said. "If a great change is needed, we will have to do what you promised," Ada said, rubbing her face against his. Arthur sighed.

"There is more to the story, Ada." The war in the sky continued raging with flashes and bangs and the land below them continued to rattle and shake. "We are not completely on our own. The moon will send us gifts from time to time that will help us become a better team. The way the others are reacting, I would not be surprised if she isn't getting ready to send one right now. She told me we would only receive and understand them when the need is great."

Ada shivered.

Off in the main group of penguins, as the heated discussion raged on and the War in the Sky and the exodus of the animals to the inland continued, the issues were crystallizing like ice.

"It seems to me," said Percy, who was a creative thinker and a sensible penguin who never let emotions carry him away, "that my father did exactly what we sent him to do. We asked him to find the Moon. He did. We asked him to request her help. He did. Apparently she agreed to help us. And she asked for something in return. That is reasonable, is it not?"

"But our wings! Flight!" moaned Roddy. "We may as well just give up right here and let those thundering beasts trample us to death. What kind of birds cannot fly? How ever will we live without flying?" (Defeatism came early and often to Roddy. When it was off taking a break, hopelessness and resignation tended to fill in.)

"Well," said Priscilla, an intelligent and earnest young penguin who was eager for the chance to try to lay her first egg and raise a hatchling, "I suppose it could be said we aren't doing a very good job of living with flying." She looked from one of their vanishingly small number to another, making especially pointed eye contact with the lady penguins.

Who began to nod in agreement.

Ethel, who was normally a very shy and serious penguin and wouldn't speak up if the sky was on fire (which, as it so happened, it was, at the moment) now injected forcefully. "It's true. My last three chicks have died in the mouths of predators. These useless wings have done nothing to spare them! If giving up my wings will let me see a chick grow into its grown-up feathers, then I can't be rid of them soon enough!" And she sang a few defiant notes to carve her opinion in ice.

"Me as well," cried Ruth, who was as outspoken and action-oriented as Ethel was timid—in other words, no shrinking sea cucumber. She was, in fact, usually the first to voice an opinion, loudly and repeatedly, and the penguin most determined to have the last word in any discussion as well. "My last egg was snatched by a skua from its nest when I was flying just a few minutes away, trying to find a bit to eat. Flying hasn't helped me one little bit."

Slowly, over the course of a couple of hours, the would-be mothers of the last penguins on Earth persuaded the whole group. The most important thing was not their wings or the flight they would be giving up. It was the chicks they would be saving.

The most important thing was their collective future.

At that point, the war in the sky seemed to reach a truce. The Moon and the Sun retreated to opposite points in the sky, and the land mass was now drifting inexorably south.

Later that evening, Arthur gathered the penguins again. He told them they should go into the sea and feed until they could feed no more, until the Moon called them. As he spoke, their wings began to recede until they were little more than tiny flippers.

The last penguins on Earth dove into the sea.

Without their long wings to drag along, they found they could swim faster and faster, dive deeper and deeper, eat more and more.

The Moon had transformed them into true creatures of the sea.

They stuffed themselves in the next few weeks with krill, growing fat and sleek. They played and did pinwheels, chasing each other through underground forests. They stayed under the surface for longer and longer periods of time, and their feathers grew denser and denser, able to keep their bodies warm under almost any circumstances.

The Moon had kept her promise.

And just as Arthur had predicted, the penguins had received the Moon's first gift just when they needed it: ***The Gift of Meaningful Purpose.***

Applying the Gift

Going from flying to swimming was a major change for the penguins.

At the outset, there were differences of opinions about the best course of action and whether it would work. It was only when they envisioned their *collective future* that the penguins could all come together in agreement. Focusing on their higher purpose, instead of what each penguin individually thought or wanted, was what enabled them to change from a group of penguins to a true team.

Many people understand *what* they do; some can explain *how* they do it; few think about *why* they do it.

Understanding your true purpose and the true purpose of your team is critical to weathering the storms and elements that are coming in your own future.

The March

What is your team's purpose?

I don't mean the mission or vision statement that is posted on your website (which, frankly, nobody really knows or understands, and which reads like the one posted by every other company out there). I mean your *true purpose* for doing what you do?

The challenge is to think about *why* you really do what you do.

When that purpose is bigger and more important than yourself, the answers will come.

CHAPTER 2
THE MARCH: THE GIFT OF EMBRACING THE UNKNOWN

In which a long and arduous march is punctuated
by The Gift of Embracing the Unknown and the
Last Penguins on Earth learn the importance of
organized activity.

The hours of sunlight grew shorter and shorter
with every passing day. The penguins fed and
swam and played until late one afternoon, almost
all at the same moment, no matter where they
were swimming, they all heard the faint call of the
Moon, telling them it was safe. It was time. They
could come back to the land.

Up they flew through the water, toward the surface,
to find floes of ice forming near the edge of the land.

Arthur, then Ada, then Percy, then Priscilla and every other penguin in turn shot out through the surface of the water and landed belly-first on the ice. It was a soft landing, because their bellies were huge from feeding. They were all twice as fat as they had ever been before.

Edmund and Roddy, who had been best pals since they were fledglings, stood back from the group, looking admiringly at a group of lady penguins. Edmund poked Roddy where his ribs should be and said, "It's a good thing I don't have to pick a lady and fly away right now, because I don't think they'd get off the ground. There's just *too much* of a good thing here! Know what I mean? Hurr hurr hurr!"

Roddy rolled his eyes and waddled away.

Around them, all the penguins found the land transformed. Ice, ice, everywhere, ice. Blinding white, wherever they turned. Above the surface of the sea, it was colder and windier than it had ever been.

For the better part of the day, penguins arrived from the water, landing on the ice from the depths of the sea.

"Well? Now what?" Edmund asked the assembled group as evening approached. (He was like that—always the penguin who was just *itching do something*, anything, *right now*.) He shrugged with his little flippers. "We certainly can't just pair up and fly off to our old nests, can we?"

Arthur, standing a little way off, looked up at the Moon, who winked and glanced down at a faraway plain, near the cave where he had found her.

He turned and said, in a clear, steady voice, "I know where we need to end up, but not how to get there, exactly. Still. Obviously, we'll have to walk."

Word spread quickly among the few hundred penguins that they should follow Arthur's lead to a new place, where they would all settle in for Egging Time.

They set off across the ice. They spread out wide and far, straggled and strayed, forming little groups as they waddled, chittering and chattering, fat and clumsy from their long weeks of gorging in the sea.

Days went by and the penguins fell into a pattern. Some waddled near the front, serious and stern. Some waddled in the middle, resolute and reliable. And some waddled around the far edges and the rear, many of them convinced penguins ought not to be walking around aimlessly on an enormous expanse of ice, because *By golly, it ain't natural.*

That's where Roddy was.

"It's a good thing we didn't have to pick a mate right away," Edmund repeated for at least the sixth time as he shuffled next to Roddy, a few groups behind from the leaders, toward the rear. "The girls just don't look the same, if you know what I mean."

Roddy scowled. It hadn't been funny the first time. Or the third. Or the fifth.

"Well, neither do you, my friend, if you don't mind me saying so," Roddy finally snapped. "If you were a chinstrap penguin you'd need seven straps by now! So don't think you're any better than any of us. We're all just great big lumps of blubber on tiny little feet now, aren't we?"

As if to add emphasis, he fluttered his now-useless

little residual wings, to show they were nearly buried in fat. The gesture threw him off balance at precisely the moment his feet encountered a clump of ice he hadn't seen looming in front of him. Without further ceremony, Roddy flopped over, face first, right onto his belly.

Edmund howled with laughter. A couple of lady penguins stopped and asked if Roddy was alright. Roddy sputtered indignantly.

"Oh, what's the use, anyway?" he wailed. "I'm as fat as a seal, I can't fly and I can barely even walk. Even if we do manage to get wherever Arthur is taking us all in one piece, what lady will want me?" Attempting to scrabble back to his feet, he let fly a great kick of frustration.

His rear claws, which had grown long and sharp during many weeks of feeding and swimming, caught the surface of the ice with precision and strength. Roddy was as surprised as anybody to find himself sailing across the ice on his belly, as if he were swimming across the surface. He swooped past several other penguins, who stopped and stared.

Edmund and the other back-stragglers nearby were caught by sheer surprise. They gathered around him.

"Roddy! How did you do that?"

Roddy wasn't sure himself, so he tried again, this time digging his rear claws into the ice intentionally and giving a strong kick. Once more, he slid forward, nearly effortlessly.

"Lie down!" he called out to the others. "It's easy! All you have to do is get on your belly and kick!" Roddy was embracing the unknown; the penguins would need to do this over and over again during their First Long Winter to learn new ways to do things when the Old Ways were no longer enough to get the job done.

If penguins were to survive, thrive and adapt to this changing land, they would need to change along with it.

During Roddy's discovery and all the ensuing excitement surrounding it, their little breakaway group of penguins (about two dozen in total) had become so engrossed in perfecting the belly slide, they completely lost track of time—and the larger migration.

The group had spent a good two hours learning the art of tobogganing—a skill that would eventually serve *all* penguins when their feet grew tired of carrying their unfamiliar and awkward weight on land.

But by the time Edmund realized they could no longer see or hear the main group, and they didn't even know which direction they should be going, it was far too late to catch up.

And the long night was falling.

————

Far ahead, at about the same time, in the slowly but steadily marching disorganized main colony, Ruth (who truth be told had a bit of a crush on Roddy) realized she could not see him anywhere in the waddling mass of birds. With a rising sense of panic, she made her way from one side of the group to the other, checking and double-checking and triple-checking. Then she began waddling quickly from the edge of all the penguins toward the center, where Arthur was trudging along, alone, a few paces ahead of the whole group. When she was close enough to call out, she cried, "Stop! Stop! Our numbers are too few! Somewhere along the way we have lost our friends!"

Penguins cannot count, really, or do any kind of mathematical calculations. So they didn't know that by the time Roddy's belly-sliding antics had peeled away the attention of the rear guard, more than 15 percent of their whole number had fallen behind.

It wouldn't have mattered anyway, because penguins don't think like that. All the penguins knew was that *every* penguin knew *some* penguin who was among the missing. And leaving them behind was not an option.

At the same time, they had already been marching for several days and were getting grumpy and impatient.

Arthur could not tell them exactly where they were going or how far away their destination was, because he had never gotten there by walking before.

To make matters worse, the lady penguins could feel that it would soon be time to make eggs, so they knew there were not many days left to get to the safe haven the Moon had promised Arthur.

What to do?

————

The Moon shone full.

A seagull cried out overhead.

Arthur looked up.

The seagull cried again.

It flew lower.

Toward Arthur.

Right at him.

"Seagull? Do I know you?" Arthur called out.

The bird circled once or twice, then landed a few feet away from Arthur.

"Well, hello again, Lucky Penguin," it said. "Again we meet. She say you might be in need of something." He spoke a language common to all the birds in the land, but with a heavy accent.

Arthur closed his eyes for a moment, silently

thanked the Moon, and nodded.

"We have lost our friends and we don't know where they are and we can't go back to find them. It is growing dark and we cannot fly. You could. You could fly and find them and lead them back to us."

"I could, Lucky Penguin, I could. Lickety split, like. But I ask, what's in it for Seagull?" The bird cooed, cocking his head to the side ever so reasonably.

Arthur was dumbfounded.

"I...I don't know. What do you want? What could we possibly have that you need?"

Here the seagull bobbed its white head before quickly replying, "Oh, you know, we never have been enemies, Lucky Penguin. I saved you from that seal, remember. Predators who take penguins are bad. Bad predators take grown, Mama and Papa penguins! But sometimes...sometimes. Sometimes are...sad things, right, Lucky Penguin? Sometimes are eggs, maybe don't hatch. Sometimes there are chicks, maybe lose their way, get separated, and can't find Mama and Papa again. Sometimes are things, sad things that happen. Sad things. Bad things. Things that mean egg won't hatch, or chick might never grow up anyway..."

Arthur understood.

These things *did* happen.

Penguins didn't like to talk about them, but they did happen.

"And you would like to...*help*." Arthur said. "With those sad things. Help *yourself*," he added, meaningfully.

"Yes, yes, help. Help you now, maybe even help them, Lucky Penguin, in a way. I promise I and my people will always make the sad things be over and done with very quick-like. We can still be friends always, still stand next to each other on the ice. We will not attack Mama and Papa penguins, never. Only help when sad things happen."

Arthur and Seagull's sad agreement, made so long ago, lives on to this very day.

———

The lost penguins were despondent. Alone on the ice in the dark and without their leader, there was squabbling and disagreement about what to do next—and whose fault it was they were in this seaweed pickle to begin with.

"We never should have let Arthur make that misbegotten deal with the Moon," Roddy grumbled. "I'd be somewhere in a nest with a nice lady penguin if it weren't for him and his newfangled ideas..."

Priscilla, who had been one of the lady penguins to stop and make sure Roddy was not hurt when he fell, fluttered her tiny wings and trilled, "Not with any of us, you wouldn't! We'd all like to have an egg that stands a chance to hatch, and to see our chicks grow up and go back to the sea. Perhaps you've forgotten the whole *point* of Egging Time, Roddy."

And the other lost lady penguins, frightened and discouraged as they were, tutted and trilled right along with her. Roddy opened his beak to argue.

"Roddy?" Edmund's voice was sharp and concerned as he stared up into the night sky. "What is a seagull doing way out here?" Roddy and all the other lost penguins turned to look at the sky in the direction where Edmund was staring.

They instinctively drew together in a tighter group. Already afraid, not knowing what to expect, cold, and losing hope, the penguins were ready for anything, including an aerial attack.

Edmund, who had to do *something*, stepped out from the group and cried up to the circling bird. "Who are you? What do you want? We are many and our beaks are sharp. We do not want trouble."

When Seagull called out from above, "I come from Lucky Arthur Penguin, to find and bring you back," their collective relief was immediate and overwhelming.

———

Seagull had not stopped to think his end of the bargain through in its entirety. Of course he could find the penguins. But bringing them back in the dead of night through the dark and the wind and the cold, keeping them together so they didn't lose anybody from this group of already lost and straggling penguins, on foot? This he had not completely planned out in advance.

"Hey penguins," he said, "Arthur ever say how he put the Moon back in sky where she belong?"

Priscilla squealed eagerly. "No, he didn't! Do you know?"

"Oh, yes, I was nearby, I saw everything. I tell you what. You penguins, you walk around me real close. Everybody listen real good. I not talk as loud as you can sing, you know, so maybe you walk a little closer than you usually walk. That way you can all hear, and nobody gets lost, ok?"

And so, as the penguins slowly walked back to their waiting friends in the dark, they heard the rest of the story, about the dinosaur and trick with the rock.

(In Seagull's telling of the story, however, he was the *real* hero.)

———

When the main migration saw the little troop of breakaways, they were initially terrified at the sight of them approaching in the distance. They could not understand why there was a giant group of seals surrounding Seagull, scooting toward the penguin colony on their bellies.

Once the two groups were reunited, there was singing and celebration in the dark, under the light of the Moon, and the lost penguins set about teaching everybody else to toboggan.

When those lessons were done, Percy let out a loud song of his own that pierced the frigid morning air. He had spent the night talking with his exhausted father, Arthur. They both knew the group couldn't withstand another episode like this one. So Percy had come up with an idea.

Friends! Friends! Gather together!

We must never part again!

As long as we walk on land

We will line up, end-to-end

Keep your eyes fixed on your leader

Keep your pace as you walk or kick

With this order and precision

We will soon be hatching chicks

The penguins couldn't argue; it was, in fact, a brilliant plan. The only question was who would line up where, and where there were minor squabbles here and there amongst the group about who would be in front or behind whom, Arthur and Percy stayed out of it, leaving it up to the penguins themselves to decide.

Three hundred penguins set off in single file from that place, and so they have marched from that day to now, to be sure no penguin gets lost or left behind.

For three more days they marched, through the lengthening nights, grateful for their new layers of fat. The cold was unrelenting. At times Arthur grew tired of leading and needed to rest. When he did, he pointed his beak where they were headed, and Percy or Roddy or another penguin took over.

As a windy morning broke on the fourth day, they saw a wall of ice rising on the horizon.

"Friends, that is it," Arthur announced. "Beyond the ice wall is a wide open plain under the cliff wall that holds the Shelter of the Moon. That plain is our place for Egging. We are almost there."

Three hundred penguins raised their heads to the sky and sang for joy.

The last penguins on Earth had set out on foot, rather than flying, into lands they had never seen from the ground, traveling in a way they had never traveled before, in a huge group instead of in single pairs, taking many days to journey over a vast unknown distances that only the previous year they could have flown in just hours, and they were refusing to lose or leave anybody behind. In their journey, they had received the Moon's second gift: *The Gift of Embracing the Unknown.*

Applying the Gift

Running toward the unknown can be both exhilarating and frightening. On the one hand, we are creatures of habit, and we tend to cling to habits and what is familiar. This makes going toward the unknown a fearful experience. On the other hand, we are also creatures who are built to take on new challenges, develop new skills and not get stuck in a rut in which we are underemployed—not using all our talents in the way we want to. There must be a balance.

I believe there are many reasons people don't embrace change and run toward the unknown. The biggest reason is fear of the consequences of failing. In order to get people to *want* to change and *want* to embrace what is new and unknown, the culture of the team has to be developed to the point where people don't fear making mistakes.

The March

Do you embrace the unknown? Do you thrive on change and trying new things, or does change bring fear and apprehension? What about your teammates?

If you all fear change, what can you do to change this? What can you bring to your team to get everybody to see beyond the temporary, the momentary mistakes and fleeting fears in order to embrace the potential of the unknown?

Companies and teams that successfully take their people to new destinations—meaning they provide new solutions for customers, new answers to their problems and new value that does not yet exist—are the ones who not only survive, but thrive when the economic storms bear down on them.

CHAPTER 3
THE PAIRING: THE GIFT OF COLLECTIVE COMMITMENT

In which the Last Penguins on Earth exercise
The Gift of Collective Commitment and pledge
themselves to pursue a joint venture to the
very end.

"Arthur?" asked Ada, staring at the flat, desolate, blinding white stretch of ice, overshadowed by a steep cliff of the same as wind picked up powdery snow and sent it swirling in little clouds here and there.

"Yes?"

"I don't understand. There are no nesting materials here. There is nothing here."

Two hundred ninety-nine penguins stared at Arthur, gobsmacked.

"That is the point. Nothing here is good. Nothing here is safe. Nothing here means no predators and no danger for our chicks. No seals will come here, that is certain. No skuas. The Moon told me we would not need nests. In fact, she said nests would be our death, because here stillness is the gravest of dangers. From now on, to live and thrive, we must move. Always."

"No nests!? How can this be?" Two hundred ninety-nine penguins spent a good few minutes expressing dismay. (This was something they were getting quite good at since the great bargain with the Moon.)

Finally, after they had grumbled themselves out, Ethel said, "Well, we are here. And there is no going back. So I am sure we will figure it out." And she waddled closer to Edmund. "Edmund? Would you like to...figure it out with me?"

Edmund bowed his head next to hers. They rubbed their faces together. For a few minutes, there was silence as they seemed to negotiate something without words.

And then, together, in unison, they raised their

beaks to the Moon and sang a song that had never been sung before.

I commit to you

By the Light of the Moon

I will move with you

I will move for you

We will make an egg

We will raise a chick

We will see it fledge

And return to the sea

I commit to this

With all I have

With my life

I commit to us

I commit to you

And so it began.

Exhausted though they were after their many-day march, the last penguins on Earth, under the shadow of a wall of ice and the protection of the smiling Moon, paired off.

Each pair invented a different song, a song created between the two of them. One hundred fifty new songs were born—one hundred fifty unique songs, all of them expressions of the commitment, solemn promises that could never be undone.

Arthur and Ada's commitment song reflected the gravity of responsibility they felt for the whole colony. The weight of the future of penguin-kind rested on their shoulders like a giant chunk of ice. While there was joy in their hearts in their choosing each other, they also knew the coming months would continue to be filled with challenges they had never faced before, and a restless, vocal group of penguins who would sometimes need to be sung down from the ledge. They pledged quiet strength to each other as well as unwavering loyalty in the face of whatever might come the penguins' way.

Percy and Priscilla's song was a joyful and short one. They were both very young, and this was their very first pairing. They just wanted to make an egg for the very first time, and their commitment was simple and pure.

Roddy and Ruth, on the other hand, had both loved and lost before. Roddy had lost two lady penguins and chicks; Ruth had lost three chicks. Their commitment song had a mournful undertone to it. They both knew sorrow and could not pretend they did not. They knew they belonged together because their hearts had holes in them. Their commitment song included a pledge to always understand the other's sadness, to give each other solace, to provide fierce protection for the egg they would make and the chick it would hatch, and a promise that even if it all ended in tears anyway ("and it probably will," moaned Roddy, silently, inward, to himself), they would remain together to the bitter end.

As the one hundred fifty songs filled the Antarctic sky, the Moon smiled.

Edmund said to Ethel, as they snuggled and listened to the others, "We were first. I'm glad. I always want us to be first. Don't you?"

Ethel snuggled back.

"Of course, Edmund. We should be first and best. At everything. Somebody has to be. Why not us?"

For four wonderful weeks, the penguin pairs shared secrets, stories and songs. Living off their fat reserves, they were losing weight, and the lady penguins were growing eggs inside of them.

Percy was the first one to notice his now-much-less-fat belly was laying on top of his feet. And unless he was mistaken, the flap of belly skin was just about the size of...an egg.

"Um, Arthur?" he asked.

"Is there something you maybe haven't told us yet?"

Indeed, there was. Arthur explained to the penguins that the mothers would need to journey back to the sea to feed.

"The Moon told me we fathers would need to be the nest for the egg."

"We what?" asked Roddy, incredulously.

"When the mothers lay the eggs, they will have to leave us almost immediately. Because they will be nearly starved. They are eating for two now—only they are eating their own blubber. See how thin they are—" (here he nuzzled Ada affectionately and protectively) "So we will need to take the egg and care for it while they return to the sea and feed."

"How?" asked Percy, clearly puzzled and concerned.

"All I know is the Moon told me the egg mustn't touch the ice," Arthur answered.

And with that, Percy went off to think.

Apply the Principle

One characteristic of high-performing teams is that they are not only comprised of a team of people who are committed, but *collectively* committed. What's the difference? Focus on the other person and the outcome for the group. It's really about *why* people are committed, not just the commitment itself. There are plenty of teams of people who don't perform that well as a unit because too many of the individuals are committed more to themselves and what they need/want than they are to what others need/want.

The March

As you look honestly at yourself and your teammates, where is your level of collective commitment? What do you need to do in order to increase this? How can you get others on your team to want to do the same? True teams are not just committed, but collectively committed. When you focus on the customer and others on your team, collective commitment thrives. This is how synergy is created and maintained. This is the team that better performing employees and better customers want to be associated with. This is The Penguin Principle.

CHAPTER 4
THE EGG: THE GIFT OF UNBREAKABLE TRUST

> In which the Last Penguins on Earth learn
> the difficult lesson of The Gift of Unbreakable
> Trust, and the tragic consequences of under-
> preparation.

Now a long darkness fell across the land. The night stretched out, and with it the deepest cold the penguins had ever felt. Storms, when they came, brought winds that felt like icy blades. To stay warm, the penguins bunched together and stood still, with their backs to the wind, creating a black wall of feathers against the onslaught of wind and snow.

By now the last penguins on Earth were all also very hungry. It had been well over six weeks since anybody had had a bite to eat.

Couples fell into comfortable silence.

———

"Edmund," Ethel whispered.

"It is here."

On her feet, under the warm pouch of skin and feathers where weeks before there had been a belly full of blubber, there peeked out the shell of one perfect, single egg.

Edmund's beak pointed straight up to the sky.

First Egg! First Egg!

The Egging Time is Here!

There were a few cries of congratulations, but other murmurs from all directions let him know the rest of the colony wasn't far behind.

Ethel lowered her head and nuzzled the egg with her beak.

"I do not want to leave," she said.

"You have to," said Edmund, "look how thin you are. Aren't you starving? Remember what Arthur said. Give me the egg. We should be first."

"Wait just a minute," Ethel protested, protective. "How are we going to do this thing? You haven't thought this through. We haven't planned, or practiced. We aren't ready. We aren't prepared."

"Just let it go, Ethel," Edmund insisted, through gritted beak. "Come on. We've done so well this far. I think we're blessed. I think the Moon wants us to be first, and she will take care of it. Just let the egg roll off your feet and it'll roll right onto mine."

"I don't think—" Ethel began.

"You don't have to think, you just have to do it!" Edmund hissed. He stepped closer to her, right in front of her, his belly touching hers.

Now Percy's voice could be heard singing, "Second Egg! Second Egg!"

And Roddy sang, "Third Egg! Third Egg!"

"Let the egg roll, Ethel!"

Edmund used his weight to bump Ethel, just a bit, to make his sense of urgency clearly felt.

Reluctantly, Ethel realized she could not reason Edmund out of the ambition to be first, and she would not have the time to break through his wall of willfulness before another couple successfully transferred their egg. If they were not the first to move their egg, then what? Would he do all he could to protect and nurture their egg if theirs were simply an ordinary egg instead of a special egg? Could she trust him to take care of the egg while she was away feeding if he didn't take extraordinary pride in their accomplishment?

Under pressure, she relented. She lifted her belly flap. The precious egg rolled forward, down, over the top of her feet, toward Edmund's feet, over a hump on her right foot, then veered to the right.

Onto the ice.

"No!" cried Edmund in horror as he scrambled after the egg, flailing at it with his shrunken winglets, which were useless. Ethel raced toward it as well, wailing in abject despair.

Edmund tried desperately to roll the egg back onto his own feet with his beak, but it tottered and spun on the ice and did not roll. Even as Edmund was trying to save the egg, Ethel could see cracks appearing in the shell. Cracks caused by the frigid temperature of the ice.

It was too late.

There would be no chick for Ethel and Edmund.

It was over. In just a matter of seconds.

Twelfth Egg!

...

Thirtieth Egg!

...

Fiftieth Egg!

...

Percy and Priscilla had spent days discussing how they would transfer the egg. They had rehearsed. They had practiced making an inverted ramp of sorts with their feet, to guide the egg very carefully from Priscilla to Percy.

And still they were terrified. But they trusted each other.

They looked into each other's eyes.

"Ready?"

"Ready."

Their clawed toes touched each other. Their beaks pointed downward as they stared intently at the egg. It rolled slowly down the channel formed by Priscilla's feet. She nudged the egg gently with her beak up the channel formed by Percy's feet and tucked it carefully into his warm, waiting pouch.

They both let out a giant sigh of relief—and realized they hadn't even known they were holding their breath.

"Go to the sea, my love, and eat," Percy said. "And be safe. Come back to us. You'll know when. The Moon will tell you."

So it was that as the mothers waddled back to the sea that first year, Edmund waddled, brokenhearted, with them.

Some say Edmund never made it.

Some say Ethel didn't, either.

But for the rest of the penguin pairs, who listened to Arthur and were careful to plan, lay their groundwork, do their homework and make sure they were fully ready for the critical moment when they traded egg from mother to father, The Gift of Unbreakable Trust was crucial to their survival.

Applying the Gift

Trust is the ultimate bond that keeps people united. The difference between Edmund and Ethel losing their egg and Percy and Priscilla keeping theirs was mutual trust. Edmund was not patient. He did not listen. Ethel did not fully trust him and the pair did not strategize the trade before the need to exchange their egg came. Percy and Priscilla were ready. They communicated, they were patient, and they planned, all because they had deep trust between them that was undeniable and unbreakable.

The March

If a true measure of trust was taken on your team, what would the results indicate? Is the level of trust among your teammates as high as it could be? If so, what got it to that point? What could make the trust levels even stronger? If it's not as high as it could be, what's keeping it down? What will you personally

commit to in order to strengthen the bond of trust
among your teammates so it is truly unbreakable?

CHAPTER 5
THE MOTHERS: THE GIFT OF SERIOUS SACRIFICE

In which the females of the Last Penguins on Earth
return to the sea, aided by an old friend.

As the very last egg was safely rolled from mother's tiny black feet to father's tiny black feet, had there been anybody else on that lonely expanse of ice, they would have heard a collective sigh of relief.

And the next thing they would have heard was a chorus of songs—goodbye songs. Because the mothers were thin as anchovies by this point, having used up their fat reserves creating these precious one hundred fifty eggs over the past six weeks, living out in the icy open, using blubber and feathers to get through the long, dark nights.

It was time for the mothers to go back to the sea and feed.

"Ada, I know you will come back to a beautiful chick," Arthur said as he gently nudged her in the direction of the water. "Go quickly, so you can get your fill of krill. We will be here waiting for you."

Ada sniffled just a little, reluctantly lowering her head to make sure the egg was tucked in safe and sound beneath Arthur's considerably larger flap of fat, then nuzzled Arthur and turned to go.

Around the colony, similar goodbyes were taking place. Edith and Edmund were nearly silent as they said their goodbyes. Percy and Priscilla were among the last to part. But eventually all the mothers were moving away, waddling as quickly as they could, tobogganing as well as they might on much tinier tummies, toward where they hoped the water they had come from was.

This, it turned out, presented a problem.

Because to get to the colony in the first place, the mothers had all been following a leader, who in turn had been following mysterious directions from somebody—or something—else.

Within a few hours of leaving the colony, the mothers realized there were no landmarks they remembered from the trip out. That long walk seemed already to have taken place a lifetime ago. They were heading back in what they hoped was the right direction...but they really would have liked to be sure.

Meanwhile, back at the colony, father penguins were getting used to the very strange feeling of being waddling incubators. Percy noticed that each step he took rotated the egg a tiny fraction and mentioned this to Arthur, who started paying attention to this as well. After a couple of hours of tiny steps and egg rotations had gone by, they had to admit it: This was a pretty good way to keep the egg uniformly warm. Because down by their feet, it was a whole lot colder than up under their belly flaps. Moving around kept the egg from catching a chill on the bottom.

Mostly, though, they slept. All the males slept. They stood in the snow, they stood in the wind, they stood in the center of the now-coldest place on the planet, and they stood in hunger. Against the rapidly deteriorating conditions in the land that was still drifting to the southernmost spot on the planet, the fathers of the Last Penguins on Earth

stood hungry and cold, and no matter what, they protected their eggs.

Out on the ice between the colony and the sea ice, Pricilla and Ada spoke in hushed tones.

"I think we are lost."

"No, I think I remember that chunk of ice..."

They looked at each other in the way young children at their first sleepover do after a very scary ghost story—trying desperately not to appear frightened, not succeeding very well, not fooling each other one little bit.

It was at that point they heard the cry of the Seagull far overhead.

"'Allo, ladies! You need help with directions again? I tell you, penguins without wings going to have to get some kind of special something to help them find their way places! Maybe that Moon, she can give you a better sense of direction!" called the Seagull.

But his was a friendly voice in an unfriendly place, and the mothers welcomed it with a chorus of welcoming cries and songs.

For several long days they walked, with Seagull telling jokes from time to time to keep their spirits up and encourage them. "Is not far now, ladies," he would say, at least once every few hours. "Water is closer now than when you left. See, days are getting longer, water is getting warmer, ice getting thinner, waves getting stronger, sea coming nearer."

So when at last the lady penguins saw the water's edge glimmering in the distance, they were overwhelmed with a combination of surprise, relief, joy, and gratitude.

"Thank you so much, Seagull," Ada said. "Please, will you fly back and tell the fathers we made it?"

"Yes, yes, in a little while, just a little while," said Seagull. "I am tired and will have a few fish now first if I can find them. Then I go."

He flew ahead toward the shore and beyond, out over the sea water, while the mother penguins finished the last few hundred yards of their long journey back to the sea.

Once they arrived, they dove headlong into the water...

...having forgotten completely about the Leopard Seals.

Seagull saw several mothers taken.

With that, his great wings beat slowly and he rose into the sky.

The surviving mothers dove deep—far deeper than the seals could follow. Their hearts were heavy, but their bellies were empty, and so they ate. But as they ate, the mothers knew they ate, not for themselves, but for all of penguin-kind. They ate so they could return over the same treacherous ground again, this time telling the fathers how to navigate the trip. They ate so they could sustain themselves and their chicks in the coming months.

Both the mothers and the fathers, in their own ways, during the first of many separations during the Egging Time, unwrapped the Moon's Gift of Serious Sacrifice. Whether it was through traveling great distances while starving and exhausted, or standing stock still for days on end against wind and cold and ice, or even paying the ultimate price in a moment of inattention, the Last Penguins on Earth did what penguins do to this very day, putting the needs of others before their own needs.

Applying the Gift

Sacrifice is not easy for anyone. By definition, it means surrendering something that is prized; in the ancient penguins' case, it was their lives. Around every corner, they had to sacrifice or they would not survive. The only way they could do this was to constantly keep their attention on their mate and the chick to come.

Focusing on other people and your purpose is the heartbeat of The Penguin Principle.

THE MARCH

Think about what it will take for you to become more successful and for your team to perform better.

What decisions do you need to make to sacrifice more? Is your sacrifice truly sacrifice, or is it merely inconvenience? There is a real difference between the two. The difference between groups, teams and tribes comes down to just a few things: one is how much each person is willing and able to truly sacrifice for the good of the others and the purpose at hand.

CHAPTER 6
THE INCUBATION: THE GIFT OF CONSISTENT ACTIVITY

In which the Last Male Penguins on Earth spend two long months keeping their eggs safe in harsh elements, receiving The Gift of Consistent Activity.

As weeks went by back at the breeding colony, the fathers had mastered the art of walk-and-roll. But everything else was increasingly challenging, as weeks without food in the half-dark went by.

The snow, the wind, and the temperatures were something they had never experienced before. And even though they had new feathers that insulated them better, even with the best insulation in the world, it isn't easy when the wind is howling at 100 miles per hour (not that the penguins knew about miles, or hours), and the temperature is -40°F (not that the penguins understood mathematical concepts like zero, or forty, or negative numbers).

The fathers were also a very loosely-organized bunch, if they were organized at all. Some would waddle off together in small groups occasionally, which always worried Arthur, who constantly felt the weight of penguinkind on his shoulders. Others seemed to need to be prodded to waddle enough.

After a while, the monotony of days and the harsh conditions inevitably began to fray at everybody's feathers. One penguin in particular who was affected was Roddy, who was never the sort of penguin to look at the bright side to begin with. But under the difficult circumstances, losing weight, being among the oldest of the penguin fathers and being very tired, there were times he became difficult to waddle with.

Today was one of them.

He was waddling with Percy and a few of the other fathers in a breakaway group out toward the edge of the colony. "I know, I know," he said, "We had to change, nothing was working anymore, had to do something different, but really, what's it all for? How are we going to raise chicks out here in this miserable spot? When we had nests, now, that was how you kept a chick warm. Are we supposed to tumble our chicks the way we're tumbling these eggs?"

The other fathers, by now used to Roddy's periods of gloom and doom, examined the sky for something interesting to remark on, and probably one of them would have liked to have said "Nice weather we're having, isn't it?" to change the subject. But it wasn't.

To tell the truth, Roddy wasn't the only penguin who was getting tired and demoralized.

"How long does it take for an egg to hatch again?" asked Frederick, one of the penguins who usually didn't say anything at all, "I didn't pay attention to those kinds of things before. Funny, the things you don't pay attention to when you're just flying around the sky, looking down on everything. Hard to believe we'll never look down on the land ever again, isn't it?"

Even Percy had to nod sadly in agreement. "Yes. Just think. Our chicks will never see the view from up there. But. We will have chicks. Someday."

"Oh, this winter! It's never going to end, is it?" Roddy was off again. "It feels like it's been a year out here in the dark already. I hope the ladies are having a good time feeding, because I am absolutely famished. And weak. Can you all feel your feet anymore?"

Frederick shook his head. "Not really. I mean, yes, technically, I can, because I can still feel the egg on top, but I can't really feel the ice below. This is a sorry life, that's for sure. But there's a reason we're doing this, remember. Feel your egg. Concentrate on your egg. Don't worry about your feet. Your feet will take care of themselves."

The group waddled in slow, slumped silence for a while.

"I mean, it's all well and good, going around, making agreements with Moons and playing tricks on dinosaurs if you're some penguins, I suppose, but who asked us?" piped Roddy again, freshened up for another round. "Nobody asked me, that's who. If my wings were any longer, I tell you, I'd have half a mind to walk over to your father, Percy, and give him a slap on the beak..."

Percy was getting ready to deliver an impassioned defense of Arthur when he felt something poke his pouch.

Poke.

There it was again.

Poke. Poke.

"Excuse me, Roddy," Percy said, steadily, but with a note of giddiness in his voice. "I think my egg is beginning to hatch."

"What ho old boy!" chirped Frederick.

"Congratulations chap!" came another exclamation.

"It won't be soon now for all of us then!"

"Why do you know, I think I may have just felt something myself!"

All around, the other fathers poured out a barrage of comments, in all sincerity, but at such a rapid-fire rate and, it must be said, at such a volume, Roddy didn't have a chance to get another word in edgewise until all the eggs were hatched in the whole colony, four days later.

And then, in the pouches, where once there had been eggs, there were the sounds of Peep! And Peep! There were downy chicks, and the fathers fed them with a special meal dispensed from a gland in their own throats.

Despite the long, hard incubation, The Gift of Consistent Activity had paid off.

Applying the Gift

I'm sure that Arthur, Roddy and the others felt like their difficulties would *never* end. I'm sure they had a hard time seeing that their reward would come. When caught in the middle of storms and difficulties, it's very hard to keep proper perspective. But their reward did come because they helped each other stay the course, mentally and physically. Their consistency paid off.

Patience pays off! Remember this: *If* you and your team are doing the right thing, stay focused, stay the course and never forget that your reward *will* come. Staying consistent in this and not wavering is not easy, but it's a characteristic of people and teams who see through their challenges long enough to collect the reward.

The March

As you think about staying consistent in your activity and your attitude, how can you make improvements? What do you need to stay more consistent in? Who can help you achieve this? Take action today to note specifics and make a commitment to seeing this through. Your reward will come.

CHAPTER 7
THE RETURN: THE GIFT OF ACTIVE LISTENING

In which the mothers and fathers of the Last
Penguins on Earth are reunited once more, a
promise made long ago is finally fulfilled, and
the importance of The Gift of Active Listening
becomes apparent.

"There! On the horizon! Do you see something?"

Percy and another group of the younger dads were
standing still, grateful not to have to be walking
anymore, nearly skin-and-bones now, as the very
last chick had hatched and they were completely
worn out. The chicks were tucked into their
belly flaps and just as warm as they could be (in
Antarctica, that is). And every beak was pointed in
the direction where their mates had disappeared so
many weeks before.

Overhead came the unmistakable cry of a Seagull. "Your Mamas, they come back to you!"

Today, every Emperor penguin sings joyfully when reuniting with a mate who has been off feeding at sea. But that year—the first year—the father penguins' songs of joy were sung louder and longer and carried over the vast distance between themselves and the penguin mothers. You could say they sang the mothers home.

And every mother left alive after the terrible ordeal of the sea and the predators sang a reply song, unique among all the others, to let her mate know she was coming.

One hundred forty-nine father penguins sang. (Obviously not Edmund, who had left long ago.)

Just one hundred thirty mother penguins sang an answering song.

The songs came in waves.

One hundred thirty fathers looked out over a sea of mothers and strained to hear one very special song. One by one, note by note, pitch by pitch, one hundred thirty fathers looked and listened.

One by one, pairs began to find each other. Ada returned to Arthur. Priscilla returned to Percy.

Roddy waddled frantically from one returning mother to another, searching face after face. "Ruth? Ruth? Have you seen Ruth? Where is she?" He asked mothers who brushed past him in their rush to find their own mates and chicks. He asked fathers who shrugged, annoyed, as they strained to hear the songs of their own mates. He rushed around the circle of penguins growing more and more desperate until he felt a tiny wing flap on his back.

It was Percy.

"Roddy, stop looking."

"But I can't find Ruth!"

"You can't find her because you are looking for her. You need to listen. Just listen. It's that simple. Where is her song? Close your eyes and listen for her song, Roddy."

And so it was that Roddy and Ruth, finally, were reunited.

One by one, listening carefully, one hundred thirty penguin fathers found one hundred thirty mothers, waddling through the swarming crowd of penguins, singing from a distance back to her, telling her whether she had a tiny little downy girl or a boy waiting in his warm, skinny pouch.

But through all this singing and all the noise, Frederick and eighteen other fathers strained to hear a song that would never come. He listened hardest of all, longer than anybody.

He continued listening even after all the singing had stopped, hoping somehow that maybe Francesca was just slower than the others, that soon she would appear on the horizon, that he would hear her song, and know that she was coming, along with the food that would feed their chick until he could return.

Finally, realizing there would be no answer to his own song, Frederick lowered his head. His shoulders drooped.

The other fathers who had heard no Mothersong had already begun filing back toward the sea. They could hold out no longer. Their fat reserves were gone. They had to eat.

"Sad time. Bad things happen," said Seagull, a few feet away from Frederick.

A few minutes later, Seagull closed the deal he had made with Arthur back outside the Moon's cave prison.

And Frederick made his way slowly away from the colony, back toward the water where they had come from.

Maybe there would be another Egging Time for Frederick, next year.

Maybe not.

Nineteen times that day, Seagull closed the deal. Again, and again, and again.

And yet, even with those losses, instead of the mere 300 penguins who had been left on Earth when Arthur had undertaken his mission to find the Moon, there were now 409.

The chicks now nestled inside their mothers' warm skin flaps. Now more songs were being sung— fervent, heartfelt goodbyes.

First the mothers sang directions to the water, including news of as many landmarks as could be picked out of a white landscape with very few distinguishing features and a tendency to be obscured by blowing snow.

The fathers listened carefully to these songs, because they would need to know the way.

Then the fathers sang their own special songs, to make sure their chicks would recognize their voices on the day of their return.

The chicks also listened carefully, because they would need to know how to recognize their fathers when they returned from the sea.

Finally, it was the chicks' turn to sing, and one hundred thirty tiny voices that had never uttered anything more complex than "peep" now trilled out their first little notes, filling the air with original compositions. Both parents listened with pride and hearts overflowing.

"I think he's going to be an especially accomplished singer," Percy said to Priscilla, as their chick finished his inaugural masterpiece. "Strong pipes on this one."

Their eyes sparkled with pride and they allowed themselves just a couple of chin-nuzzles.

Then the remaining starving, exhausted fathers who had not already abandoned the colony turned, en masse, back to the nourishing icy Antarctic seas.

Seagull, by now a familiar presence, tagged along, telling jokes to try to bolster the fathers' exhausted, flagging spirits and worn-out bodies.

And even though Seagull had fed just hours before on motherless chicks, the father penguins bore him no ill will. They knew the chicks were doomed without mothers and could not begrudge Seagull a meal, no more than they could be angry at the leopard seals who had taken the mothers.

This was simply the nature of life, and the necessity of nourishment. Surely krill had family too, when you stopped to think about it? And one day after a penguin had come through the kelp bed at the bottom of the sea, a mother krill would find herself alone without father krill?

These things happened before the deal outside the Moon's prison cave. They would continue to happen afterward.

The deal with Seagull was just...a special arrangement.

It took the fathers fewer days to get back than it had even taken the mothers to get to the colony, because the sea was returning and overtaking the sea ice. The weather was warming.

Roddy was starving.

Just a few feet from the sea, he was about to hurl himself into a rapid toboggan and face-plant into what he imagined to be a smorgasbord of krill.

"Roddy!" Arthur shouted. "Stop!"

Having been briefed on the tragedy of the Leopard Seals, Arthur had a request.

"Seagull? Would you please take that very full belly of yours and do a flyover of the water? We would like to know if you see anything lurking just under the ice...and if so, where."

Seagull had to admit, it was a fair request.

And so it was that all of the fathers of the Last Penguins on Earth all made it safely into the water, and the Leopard Seals found themselves wondering how one hundred forty-nine penguins managed to elude them and dive quickly to maximum depth, where they were now safe to gorge on Mr. and Mrs. Krill for the next few weeks, fattening up for the next round of chick-sitting.

By the time the fathers returned to that ancient Antarctic rookery, well-fed and fat, several remarkable things had happened.

For one thing, the chicks were scampering about on the ice, out of their mothers' pouches, playing with each other in groups supervised by a watchful mother or two. And it became apparent that the chicks, too, had learned to listen carefully.

Percy learned this when he approached the colony singing and was greeted at the edge of the rookery first, not by Priscilla, but by his daughter, who flitted up to him, was beating her tiny wings excitedly and trilling her own song, which of course he recognized instantly.

"Well, greetings again, my tiny little egglet! I never would have recognized you without your beautiful singing!" Percy laughed, singing right back at her. Pricilla joined them a few moments later. She was not quite as thin this time, so they might have a few extra minutes before they had to say goodbye again.

"I'm not an egglet, I'm Petunia!" their daughter squeaked.

"And she's definitely her father's daughter," Priscilla whispered to Percy as the pair rubbed chins in an emotional greeting. "Clever, headstrong, independent and you never know what she's going to be getting up to next. Keep an eye on this one while I'm gone."

All across the colony, fathers were meeting and learning the names of the chicks they had so lovingly incubated and hatched.

"Arthur, this is Ansel, your son," said Ada.

"Pleased to make your formal acquaintance," said Arthur," bowing, and his chick bowed back, very stiffly.

"He's been practicing that for weeks," Ada said. "He is a very proper young penguin, you see."

"Tell me, Ansel, what do you do when you aren't practicing your bowing?"

"I like to play ice-kick with the boys," said Ansel.

"Ice-kick, eh? That sounds like fun. Could you show me later? As soon as your mother has gone? I'd like to see this game."

"Yes, Papa, I would like that." Ansel was much more relaxed talking about ice-kick.

"But first let me hear your song, so I'll know where to find you just in case your game of ice-kick takes you to the other edge of the colony, OK?"

Ansel giggled. "I don't sing too well, Papa, but…" And then he sang. He was right. He didn't sing too well.

But if he were anything like his father and mother, he would probably make up for his lack of singing talent in other ways—like diplomacy and leadership.

And so, likewise, Georgina introduced George to Godric.

Clara introduced Clarence to Clancy.

Ruth introduced Roddy to Rudy.

Ella introduced Ellsworth to Emma.

And so on, and so forth, until all the offspring and all the fathers had made a proper acquaintance, and the mothers had set off to sea once more. The fathers let them know it was now just a few short days' journey back to the sea, with the weather so relatively warm and fine and the sea so close.

The Moon's Gift of Careful Listening had been bestowed.

As Arthur, Percy, Roddy, Clarence, George, Ellsworth, and the rest of the one hundred thirty father penguins stood and watched groups of thirty or forty growing chicks organized themselves to play ice-kick, they could have been forgiven for thinking the worst was behind them.

Applying the Gift

In order to find their mates, penguins—even today—have to listen. They don't rely on sight, but on sound—specific sound. Yes, in order to hear their mate's song, the penguins must be very active listeners, taking this skill to an exquisite level of concentration.

What about you and your team? How well do you listen, really listen? I see too many business people, especially salespeople, go through the motions of listening, but not really performing active listening.

The difference between the two comes down to one thing: listening to *understand* what the other person is saying *without the intent to reply.* This requires putting what you want to hear aside while you focus on the other person and what they have to say.

That's The Penguin Principle. When you do this, you'll discover opportunity you didn't realize existed. You'll be respected, valued and looked at as a partner instead of a vendor. Now isn't that a better way to do business?

The March

As you encounter various discussions today, take your active listening to another level. Don't just hear them; listen to them. Ask better questions. Read between the lines of what they're saying. Put aside your intent to reply. Get to their truth. This is the bedrock of any great relationship.

CHAPTER 8
THE STORM: THE GIFT OF CREATIVE INNOVATION

In which the Sun, having long plotted her revenge, tries to execute it, and things look very bleak indeed for the Last Penguins on Earth and their chicks.

The Storm began just as Seagull was ushering the mothers safely into the sea.

The Sun's warm rays, which had glinted off the small chunk of ice the chicks were kicking around, trying to keep it away from the opposing team and sneak it past a designated "guardian," disappeared suddenly behind rapidly gathering storm clouds. The chicks and their fathers looked up, wondering what could have brought on dusk so quickly in the midday.

What they saw was terrifying.

Black roiling clouds that looked like dark ocean waves, only in the sky, were pouring down over the peaks of the mountaintops, heading straight for the colony.

At the same time, they could hear a howl made up of many howls all at once—low, high, mid-register—the howl of winds of every speed, winds high in the clouds, low on the ground, winds blowing up, winds blowing down, winds slicing across the land from every direction.

Arthur and Percy and Ellsworth and Roddy and George and the rest of the fathers scrambled to surround the chicks, who needed no urging to come in from their creches and gather into a tight huddle. The fathers, completely overwhelmed, unprepared, having faced nothing like this in their experience ever before, could do nothing but pull their bodies together and face their backs to the onslaught. When the snow came—and it came quickly—it took only minutes for the ferocity of the wind-driven sheets of flakes to turn their black backs white. It was becoming clear that if they just stood there, the fathers would freeze to death in short order—and the chicks would follow.

It would all have been for nothing.

This Storm was not a natural storm.

It was a storm the Sun had sent to punish the penguins for helping the Moon. It was a storm like no other storm in Antarctica, before or since.

Some say that Storm created the glaciers that cover the whole continent to this day.

That is how mighty, how terrible, how awesome that Storm of Wind and Snow and Cold sent by the Sun was, when she turned her back on Antarctica for a full week.

The mothers were all gone, feeding once more. The fathers couldn't hold out much longer. Their feathers were heavy with snow, and their strength was failing under the onslaught of wind. The chicks, too big to hide in pouches anymore, too young to survive the terrors of the storm much longer, too vulnerable and inexperienced to have any idea what to do, were paralyzed with terror.

Percy, standing next to Arthur, heard Arthur's breath begin to fail. His own vision was beginning to fail.

"Arthur," Percy said. "Tell us one last time about the Moon. Tell us what she promised."

"I guess...she...did...all...she could…" Arthur gasped. It was clear he was near the end of his tether, physically, emotionally and in all other ways.

Percy closed his eyes. All of his best ideas came to him when his eyes were closed. He never knew why—he only knew that was how it worked.

"What if we formed a great huddle around the chicks?" he shouted.

"That would work for a little while," Roddy yelled back, "But then all of the penguins on the outside of the huddle would freeze like stones, and all the penguins on the inside would be trapped."

Percy thought some more.

"What if we laid in a mound with the chicks at the center? The fathers might not all make it but the chicks would. They are old enough to take care of themselves with just a few of us to watch over them now. I am willing to make the sacrifice and be at the bottom or the top of the mound," Percy said, grimly. And nobody doubted his word.

Arthur looked at his son with an overwhelming combination of tenderness and admiration. "If…if it comes to that, Percy, I will join you."

Percy closed his eyes again and he pictured their benefactor. And in his mind's eye, he saw the Moon in the sky. He pictured her trajectory through the sky through the seasons. He saw in his mind's eye how, as the weeks and months passed, she began her journey low on the horizon one night, then rose higher in the sky the next night, higher still the next night, higher the next. She would look like a crescent one night, and be fuller the next, fuller the next, until she shone full, then became an oval, waning, waning, waning, until she was a crescent again. And as she went through her phases, she moved lower, lower, lower in the sky.

The moon was always moving around the Earth, Percy realized. The path she took across the sky was a spiral. She was spiraling through the sky.

"Arthur! Boys! What if we move like the Moon? What if we move in a spiral, and everybody churns into and out of the center? That way nobody will have to bear the full brunt of this storm? The Moon showed me what we need to do! We have to

move in a spiral! We have to move like the Moon!"
Percy's cries pierced even the howling of the wind.

Percy knew every penguin's life depended on their
hearing and understanding the message he had just
received from the Moon, and acting upon it quickly.
But how to get it out in this howling awful storm?

"Arthur," he said to his failing father," "I need you
to help me rally them one last time. I need you to
do this or it's over. Can you do something? Can
you sing?"

Arthur could barely open his eyes by now. But he
nodded.

"Good. Here is the message."

To the right and in, Fathers,

to the right and in

Slowly walk to the right and in

Leave the chicks in the center

We encircle them

Carry this message to the right and in

When you get to the center

Move to the left and out

When you get to the edge

Go to the right and in

Sing until you get to the edge again

We are spiraling against the Storm

Arthur heard. And he understood it was a message from the Moon. This broke through his fatigue and despair. And so he sang to the penguin on his right, as he began to move, and the bird on his right began to sing and move, and slowly, the first Great Spiral of penguins began.

The result was, of course, a huge, ever-moving, ever-changing mass of birds that maximized warmth, minimized exposure of any one bird to the punishing storm, protected the chicks, and prevented the penguins being buried under mountains of snow.

Just under the horizon, the Moon smiled. She had delivered her Gift of Creative Innovation.

Applying the Gift

Around every corner, every team faces storms that come in all sizes, all shapes and usually in the colors black and white. Teams that weather them better than others are those who collaborate creatively.

What does that mean in plain English? It means that the team is made up of people who possess that balance to feel free to be themselves, often coming up with great ideas, but who also act collectively, meaning they are willing to put aside what they want if it's not in the group's best interest.

The March

What storms are bearing down on your team right now? Do team members, including you, feel like you can be yourselves and come up with creative solutions to weather them better? Are team members, including you, willing and able to put your desires, ideas and plans aside if it's not in the best interest of the team? Apply this to a specific situation that you are in right now and come up with a creative solution to weather your storm. The answer is closer than you think.

CHAPTER 9
THE GREAT SPIRAL: THE GIFT OF THE TRUE TRIBE

In which the Last Penguins on Earth pull together and receive The Gift of the True Tribe and learn the lesson of selflessness in their last desperate bid for survival.

Some penguins, of course, had a harder time than others in the spiral, simply because this Storm was no natural storm.

Roddy wanted to lie down at one point. "Just for a moment," he said. "Just to get some rest."

The spiral wasn't stationary. By its nature, it was also drifting across the expanse of ice where the rookery had made its home. Arthur stayed back with Roddy, desperate not to lose another bird this late in the game.

"Roddy, we have been through so much. You can't lie down. If you lie down, you will freeze to death. You have to continue. This spiral group is our only safety. It is our only warmth. It is our only shelter," Arthur pleaded.

"For the love of the Moon, Roddy, get up and come with me." Already snow was building up on both their feathers and the nearest arm of the spiral was getting difficult to see as the snow and the driving wind obscured the backs of the receding larger group of penguins.

"Arthur, I appreciate everything you have done, but I am just exhausted," Roddy said. And he meant it. "I don't think I can continue."

He flopped onto the ice. He panted. His eyes closed.

"You might not think so," said Arthur. "But Ruth and Rudy would want you to. Rudy is in the spiral even now. Can you continue for them? Think about what we have all been through up to this point. Think about our purpose, Roddy. We are not just a group of penguins moving across the ice; we are the cornerstone of generations of penguins to come. Don't quit now."

Rudy groaned.

Arthur knew he had hit perhaps Roddy's last functioning nerve.

"Just one more moment," Roddy shouted above the wind.

"Another moment and you will never stand up again."

Then Roddy pulled himself, heavily, laboriously, exhaustedly to his feet, shook the snow off his body, opened his eyes, looked into Arthur's, and said, simply, "Thank you. Thank you for keeping me on track. Thank you for reminding me that going on is our purpose. Thank you for helping me to focus and find my second wind."

The two of them set off to catch up with where they thought the spiral was.

Which turned out not to be where it actually was.

Or maybe they were moving more slowly than they thought they were, on account of the depth of the snow, and the wind being in their faces, against them.

Surely they had only been out of the spiral for a minute, two minutes tops.

Surely they should already have caught back up with the spiral of penguins.

Surely they should be able to see some black somewhere in the screaming, wailing wall of whiteness, this neverending storm...

"I am sure it's just up ahead, Arthur," Roddy said.

Arthur's breathing was labored again. He was not—and many penguins forgot this from time to time—he was not the youngest penguin in the colony. He was old enough to have a breeding son. Old enough to have known about the war between the Sun and the Moon. Old enough to have known to strike out in search of the Moon in the first place.

Old enough to have known better than to have left the safety of the spiral.

"Arthur. Arthur, we will find them. Keep marching, Arthur. Steady. Slow and steady, Arthur," said Roddy, peering ahead, leading the way, now, keeping track of Arthur's whereabouts by listening for the heavy breathing behind him. 'We are going to find them. You stayed behind for me, Arthur, and I will not let them lose you. You are too important to them. To all of us. You saved my life that day at the water, the day you sent Seagull over the water to look for seals. I never really thanked you for that. Well, today I am. Today I will get you back to all the others. We are going to find that spiral."

He was speaking as much for his own morale as he was for Arthur's at this point.

And then it occurred to him.

Don't look. Use your song.

"Hello? Is there anybody listening?" he sang, as loudly as he possibly could.

"We are here," answered Percy's voice, just a few dozen yards away.

So it was that Arthur saved Roddy, and Roddy saved Arthur, and they were both fast-tracked to the center of the spiral to get warm again.

In the spiral, during the Great Storm, that very first winter, the penguins unwrapped The Gift of True Tribe, becoming a huge, selfless network of penguins working as one, toward a common goal.

No individual penguin is ever thinking of his or her own needs in the spiral. The spiral is more than the group. It is a tribe in which each member is focused 100 percent on each other, not themselves, galvanized around their purpose. They are not just moving forward; they are a movement unto themselves.

The spiral is The Penguin Principle at its pinnacle.

Applying the Gift

True teamwork is not just a collective group moving forward, but rather a collective group that forms a movement.

A team is a group of people moving forward, producing outputs, measured in many ways. The focus is on the *return* on investment. A tribe is a group of people who are a movement, producing impact, some of which can be measured and some not. The focus is on the *recipients* of investment.

The difference between a team and a tribe comes down to one simple thing: teams focus on

THE **PENGUIN PRINCIPLE**

themselves; tribes focus on others. Teams agree with *The Penguin Principle*; tribes live it.

The March

In your current situation, are you a team or a tribe? What is the gap that's bridging the two? More important, what will *you* do and what else can the others do in order to become a true tribe? Most important, what will be the lasting impact?

CHAPTER 10
THE FLEDGLINGS: THE GIFT OF LASTING LEGACY

In which the No-Longer-Last-Penguins-on-Earth,

to celebrate the fact that they have overcome

all odds and raised their chicks successfully,

pass along a song about what it means to be a

penguin, then, now and forever.

Although it seemed as though it never would, the storm ended. Whether the Moon finally had a word with the Sun to bring that about, nobody will ever know.

What we do know is this: Seagull came to the colony, once it was all over, with a message for Arthur from the Moon.

"Those two sisters, they don't like each other, and they may not like penguins. But they see what you do. They see you all very brave. Sun, Moon, they say, never again, no more. Is done. No more war. No more big battles. Moon stay on her side, her season, long nights. Sun stay on her side, her season, long days. No more. That's what they say."

Arthur considered.

"Do you believe them?"

"Moon never lied to me. Ever lied to you?"

"Now that you put it that way, no. No, the Moon did everything she promised me. And then some. Thank you, Seagull, for bringing us the news."

Seagull looked out over the colony, which by now was practically on top of the rapidly advancing sea.

"Handsome chicks, all got their pretty black feathers now," said Seagull. "Not even chicks no more, practically grown up, big like you and the Mamas. You teach them to swim?"

Arthur laughed. "I don't think we'll need to teach them to swim. They'll be heading into the water on their own any day now. It's part of being a penguin. After all, did anybody have to teach you to fly?"

Seagull laughed right back.

They watched a few of the fledglings playing ice-kick. Most of the other adults were already spending parts of their days in the water, diving for krill, making the colony emptier than it usually had been.

"Do you miss it? To fly?" asked Seagull.

Arthur didn't look away from the youngsters. "Every day," he said. Then quietly added, "and I don't regret it for a second. I don't think you'll find a Mama or Papa penguin who would answer differently."

"Well, I don't care what they say. You the very special penguin who talk to the Moon, Arthur," said Seagull. "Maybe for your trouble, the others, they should make you Emperor of the penguins!"

"I don't think so," Arthur laughed. "We don't need any Emperors."

He watched happily as more than a hundred nearly-grown fledgling offspring of the No-Longer-Last Penguins on Earth spent one of their final joyful youthful sunsets, playing near the sea.

"And that, my little ones, is the story of the Penguin Principle," finished the modern-day penguin mother, as the group of rapt fledglings stared at her with wide-open eyes and wide-open beaks.

"But we are Emperor penguins, Mama!" said a clever young fledgling. "So Seagull was right! Arthur really was the Emperor of penguins, wasn't he?"

"I suppose he was, little one. I suppose he was. Now. Who's up for a game of ice-kick?"

Twelve million descendants of Arthur, Ada, Percy, Priscilla, Roddy, Ruth and all the Last (Emperor) Penguins on Earth live in Antarctica today, and they return, every year, to the same rookeries where they were hatched themselves, year after year, reliving every breeding season the same rituals and habits that were born of the gifts of the Moon.

Facing nearly the same conditions in the very first year that things changed forever, living much as the Last Penguins on Earth did, today's Emperor penguins, like the brave penguins of Arthur's little band, continue to work together selflessly in the harshest place on Earth as a result of the Moon's final gift: The Gift of Lasting Legacy. All

their sacrifice, selflessness and collaboration built something unimaginable: a thriving population of descendants who carry on their traditions to this very day.

After the tale was over, but before their game of ice-kick, the modern-day fledglings might have sung a song composed on the Antarctic ancient ice by Petunia, Percy and Pricilla's musical prodigy, which is known to all Emperor penguins, even to this day:

What is The Penguin Principle?

We give all we have.

To whom do we give it?

Each other, even before ourselves.

Why?

So there may always be penguins,

every season,

one after the other,

for all the seasons

of all time.

Applying the Gift

Legacy is like purpose on steroids—it's bigger, it's stronger and it's permanent. Legacy is the last chapter in each of our lives; the one people will likely remember us by.

My question for you is this: If your book ended today, how would the last chapter read? What lasting message and impact would it have on the people who come after you, forever?

More importantly, what *can* you and *will* you do to create a legacy that you really want? What will it take to achieve this?

I know for every person reading this story, the answers to these questions vary tremendously. However, the one constant is this: In order to create an *intentional* legacy that you really want, and to make the right kind of lasting impact forever, it's going to take living *The Penguin Principle* every day.

The March

Immediately after finishing this book, take five minutes to reflect. Go somewhere that is quiet;

somewhere without a smartphone disturbing you; somewhere where you can really discover your *first* step to living *The Penguin Principle.*

Then, *write down your answer* and *make a commitment* to taking a specific plan of action.

If you need help following through on your march, find someone who can walk by your side— somebody who can encourage you, whom you can confide in to see this through.

Your own march can change your life and potentially the lives of countless others forever to come.

ACKNOWLEDGEMENTS

The Penguin Principle is dedicated to all the people who want to raise their standard of conduct and their level of impact. My hope is that this story will help you focus much more on other people and what they want and need. Look at what you want and need as a byproduct of living The Penguin Principle. When you do, you'll find that your reputation and the word of others will work much harder for you than your own direct efforts. In the end, you'll not only have much more of what you want and need, in addition, you'll have purpose and meaning that money can never buy.

A special thank you to Henry DeVries, an amazing publisher, and Denise Montgomery, the best creative consultant and editor, who brought this concept to life.

To all my customers who have supported me over the years, thank you for allowing me to bring stories from Antarctica to you and your teams.

To Greg Godek, who convinced me to go to Antarctica in 2005.

Most of all, the biggest thank you goes to my wife, Angela Pierce, who has stood by my side for more than twenty-five years and counting. Thank you Angela. I love you more than words could describe.

ABOUT THE AUTHOR

In January 2006, Mike became one of nine people to have run a marathon on the Antarctic continent. Eleven months later he returned to Antarctica to become the first American to complete the Antarctic Ultra Marathon, a grueling 100 kilometers (62.1 miles). Since then Mike has completed many other winter marathons in the coldest and harshest climates on earth. His stories have been featured in *Sports Illustrated* and on CNN, Fox, ABC, CBS, ESPN, and many other national and international media outlets.

OK, you're thinking: *Why?* Surprisingly, it has very little to do with cold weather or sports. Rather, it's about the disciplines necessary to be successful in difficult situations. Teams today face the same challenges as those who first conquered Antarctica. The question is this: Are we ready?

The Penguin Principle is all about one thing: true teamwork. The Emperor penguins in Antarctica are the only living creatures who can withstand the harshest conditions on earth. They do so because they operate like a true team, not just a group. *The Penguin Principle* will look closely at a number of elements that high performing teams can incorporate into their day to day operations in order to function at the highest levels, no matter what the circumstances.

Mike holds his BA in Marketing from the University of Colorado, Boulder and resides in Encinitas, California with his wife Angela.